GREYSCALE

FAIRIES & Angels

BARBARA LANZA

Fairies & Angels
Copyright © 2017 by Barbara Lanza
All rights reserved
www.barbaralanza.com
blanza@optonline.net
Fairy Lane Books

Dedication

Miranda McGrath & Juanjo Auve
with love always

Colored by

Fairies and Angels contains 25 greyscale pictures to
color. Seven pictures are of angels and the remaining
are of fairies.
The paper is not bleed proof, so please place a heavier
piece of paper under the page when using markers.
It is hoped that coloring this world adds more serenity to yours.

Barbara

www.ingramcontent.com/pod-product-compliance
Lightning Source LLC
Chambersburg PA
CBHW081153040426
42445CB00015B/1864